GOLF

BY BRIAN HOWELL

CONTENT CONSULTANT
WARD CLAYTON
GOLF COMMUNICATIONS/PUBLIC RELATIONS PROFESSIONAL

Printed in the United States of America,
North Mankato, Minnesota
102011
012012

 THIS BOOK CONTAINS AT LEAST 10% RECYCLED MATERIALS.

Editor: Chrös McDougall
Copy Editor: Anna Comstock
Series Design and Cover Production: Craig Hinton
Interior Production: Kelsey Oseid and Marie Tupy

Photo Credits: Eric Risberg/AP Images, cover (bottom); Dustin Steller/iStockphoto, cover (top); Phil
Sandlin/AP Images, 1; Amy Sancetta/AP Images, 5, 49, 59 (bottom); Elise Amendola/AP Images, 6;
Dave Martin/AP Images, 9; Mark J. Terrill/AP Images, 10; Alastair Grant/AP Images, 13, 58 (middle);
Gerhard Hoornbach/The British Library/Heritage Images, 14, 58 (top); Sarah Fabian-Baddiel/
Heritage Images, 20, 58 (bottom); Lyon and Turnbull/AP Images, 23; Horace Cort/AP Images, 27; AP
Images, 28, 31, 32, 35, 37, 41, 43, 59 (top), 59 (middle); Harry How/Getty Images, 44; Chris O'Meara/
AP Images, 47; Evan Vucci/AP Images, 53; Martin Rickett/PA Wire/AP Images, 54; Rebecca Naden/
PA Wire/AP Images, 57

Library of Congress Cataloging-in-Publication Data
Howell, Brian, 1974-
  Golf / by Brian Howell.
    p. cm. -- (Best sport ever)
  Includes index.
  ISBN 978-1-61783-143-0
  1. Golf--Juvenile literature. I. Title.
  GV968.H69 2012
  796.352--dc23
                        2011033781

TABLE OF CONTENTS

CHAPTER 1

GREEN JACKET FOR LEFTY

P hil Mickelson positioned his club behind the golf ball. He
set his feet and took one last look at the hole, which sat
18 feet (4.49 meters) away. The left-handed Mickelson—who is
nicknamed "Lefty"—drew back his putter and gave the ball a tap.
As soon as he did, the crowd that surrounded the green stood
and roared. "Get in the hole!" many of them shouted as the ball
inched its way along the green.

Mickelson's body did not move and his head barely turned as
he watched the ball roll. All around him, anticipation grew. His
wife, Amy, held hands with other family members. The game of
golf has produced some remarkable moments throughout the
years. This was one of them.

Phil Mickelson swings on the first fairway during the 2004 Masters.

Phil Mickelson celebrates his first major championship after sinking his final putt to win the 2004 Masters.

Few golfers in recent history have been as popular as Mickelson. He is a down-to-earth family man. Mickelson is a fan favorite at every tournament. This was no ordinary tournament, though. This was the Masters Tournament. Known by many simply as the Masters, it is one of the most prestigious tournaments in golf.

Professional golf tournaments take place in different parts of the world nearly every week. But four tournaments stand above the rest. The Masters, the US Open, the British Open, and the Professional Golfers' Association of America (PGA)

Championship are known as golf's four majors. To truly be considered a great player, golfers believe they need to win these events.

Despite his successes in other tournaments, Mickelson went into the 2004 Masters without a victory in a major tournament. Many people considered him perhaps the best player to never win a major. But as that 18-foot putt rolled toward the final hole on that April afternoon in Augusta, Georgia, that was about to change.

The ball kept rolling. The crowd kept roaring. When the ball finally disappeared into the cup, the crowd erupted in a loud cheer. Mickelson recorded a birdie. That meant he scored 1 shot under par for the hole. That result was good enough to win the tournament by 1 stroke. Mickelson raised both of his arms in the air and jumped. Finally, he had done it!

THE PUTTER

The putter is one of the more specialized—and most important—clubs in a golfer's bag. Each club is designed to hit different types of shots on a golf course. Players use the putter to finish each hole. Unlike other clubs, the putter generally has a flat surface. There is also very little loft to the putter, compared to other clubs. In addition, a putter sometimes has a line grooved or drawn onto the top. This allows the players to line up their ball before they hit. How a player performs with the putter can often determine how they finish. Phil Mickelson was great with his putter when he won the 2004 Masters. At the 2011 Masters, however, Mickelson said it was his failure to do well with the putter that caused him to finish in a tie for 27th place.

Champion at Last

Before the 2004 season, Mickelson had played in 46 majors. He had finished second in majors three times. He also had five third-place finishes in majors. Four of those had occurred at the Masters. Mickelson had been so close to winning a major in the past that he almost could not believe it when he finally did win. Shortly after his final putt, he picked up his daughter, Amanda, and said, "I did it! I won! Can you believe it?!"

At the awards ceremony, Mickelson was given a coveted green jacket. The forest-green sport coat is presented to the winner of the Masters each year. It is tradition at the Masters for the previous year's winner to slip the green jacket onto the back of the current winner. Mike Weir had won the 2003 Masters. He placed the green jacket on Mickelson.

"It was an amazing, amazing day, the fulfillment of all my dreams," Mickelson said after his win.

AUGUSTA NATIONAL

Every year since 1934, the Masters has been played at Augusta National Golf Club in Augusta, Georgia. Augusta National has become known as one of the greatest and most sacred golf courses in the world. The course has several famous holes. Some of them are in the "Amen Corner." It covers holes 11, 12, and 13. The area was given that name by *Sports Illustrated* writer Herbert Warren Wind in 1958. He borrowed the nickname from an old jazz music tune called, "Shoutin' in that Amen Corner." Wind felt those holes featured some of the most important play during the 1958 Masters.

Phil Mickelson, *left*, became only the second left-handed golfer to win the Masters. Mike Weir, *right*, the 2003 winner, was the first.

Winning the 2004 Masters was just the beginning for Lefty. Through the 2011 season, he had won four major championships. That included two more wins at the Masters, in 2006 and 2010.

A Favorite for Fans

The opportunity and desire to see Mickelson win attracted a lot of fans to the 2004 Masters. Mickelson is one of many golfers who has been a fan favorite throughout the years. Bobby Jones, Walter Hagen, and Gene Sarazen were stars in the 1920s. Ben Hogan, Byron Nelson, and Sam Snead dominated in the 1930s,

US golfer Paula Creamer has been among the most popular female golfers since she turned pro in 2004.

1940s, and 1950s. Arnold Palmer came along in the 1950s and 1960s. Then Jack Nicklaus dominated in the 1960s and 1970s.

Today, Mickelson, Tiger Woods, Ernie Els, Jim Furyk, Rory McIlroy, Vijay Singh, and Lee Westwood are among the most popular male golfers in the world. Paula Creamer, Cristie Kerr, Morgan Pressel, Karrie Webb, Michelle Wie, and Yani Tseng are among the most popular female golfers. Those men and women are also among the most famous—and highest-paid—athletes in all of sports. In 2010, Woods and Mickelson were the two highest-paid US athletes.

THE GREEN JACKET

One of the most unique aspects of the Masters is the green jacket awarded to the winner. During the 1930s, members of the exclusive Augusta National Golf Club wore the green jacket as a sign that they were someone to ask for tournament information. It later became a symbol for the prestigious tournament. The legendary Sam Snead was the first player awarded a green jacket when he won the Masters in 1949.

Golf has a special connection between its fans and its stars. Unlike some of the popular team sports, golf is a game that can be played by anyone. More than 26 million Americans played golf in 2010. Many recreational golfers identify with the stars of their sport. The average golfer can recognize the ability it takes to win the Masters and other professional tournaments. In addition, golf has become a passion for many fans because they have the opportunity to watch their heroes for years. The top professional golfers often play for decades.

At the 2011 Masters, the 71-year-old Nicklaus and 81-year-old Palmer hit ceremonial tee shots to start the 75th playing of the event. Years removed from competition, Nicklaus and Palmer were still as popular as they were 50 years earlier when they were the dominant players.

THE EARLY DAYS

Winning a golf tournament is not an easy task. It takes several days of good play to finish on top. Winning a tournament on the Old Course at St. Andrews in Scotland might be one of the toughest tasks in all of golf.

For more than 600 years, golfers have taken their turn at the Old Course. Because of its difficulty, not everyone loves it. But many of the game's all-time greats have found a place in their hearts for the course.

"If I had ever been set down in any one place and told that I was to play there, and nowhere else, for the rest of my life, I should have chosen the Old Course at St. Andrews," said Bobby Jones. He won the British Open at St. Andrews in 1927.

Tom Watson waves to the crowd from the famous Swilken Bridge at the Old Course at St. Andrews during the 2010 British Open.

Golf in some form has been played in Scotland since the fifteenth century.

The British Open rotates among different courses in Great Britain each year. Tom Watson won the event five times in his career. But he never could win it at St. Andrews. Still, he had fond memories when he played at St. Andrews in 2010.

"St. Andrews, when I first played here, I didn't like it," Watson said. "But I learned to like it. And, eventually, to love it."

The Home of Golf

Golfers grow to love the Old Course because it holds so much history. Nobody really knows when or where golf was first played. Games similar to golf can be traced back hundreds of years to places such as Japan, China, and the Netherlands.

It is Scotland, however, that generally gets credit for being golf's birthplace. In particular, St. Andrews is recognized as the home of golf. The Scottish course has been in use since the early 1400s, although its official charter was established in 1552.

"The Scots were the first to play a game in which the players used an assortment of clubs to strike a ball into a hole dug in the earth," according to golf writer Herbert Warren Wind. "This is the essence of the game we know as golf. It is generally accepted that golf is the product of Scotland."

Golf was already a popular game during the mid-1400s. In fact, it was so popular that King James II of Scotland banned the game. The king believed that playing golf prevented men from practicing their archery. They needed to be good archers to prevent the English from invading their country.

18 HOLES

A standard round of golf consists of 18 holes. For many years, a round at the Old Course at St. Andrews in Scotland had 22 holes. In 1764, however, the course was reduced to 18. Golfers at St. Andrews believed that several of the holes were too short. Therefore, some of the holes were combined, and the final number was 18. Because of that change, 18 became the standard.

King James III and King James IV both upheld the ban. Finally, in 1502, King James IV changed his mind and lifted the ban. And he actually became a golfer himself. One of the first female golfers was Mary Stuart. She was commonly known as Mary, Queen of Scots. James IV and Mary are among the most famous people to ever play at the Old Course at St. Andrews.

During golf's early years, players looked more like they were going to work or church than out to the golf course. Players wore long-sleeve dress shirts, woolen sport coats, and even ties. Players also wore knickers. They are loose-fitting short pants that are bunched at the knees. Many players wore the same type of clothing off the course.

The game continued for hundreds of years without any formal rules. The Honourable Company of Edinburgh Golfers established the first set of rules in 1744. There were 13 rules.

THE BALL

During most of the 1800s, a golf ball was made out of leather stuffed with feathers. During the process in which a ball was made, the leather and feathers were wet. Later, once they dried, the feathers inside expanded and the leather shrank. That created a hard ball to hit. In 1898, Coburn Haskell and Bertram G. Work received a patent for a new ball. It consisted of rubber thread wrapped around a rubber core. Golf balls are still made of those materials.

Many of them are still in place. Among them is the rule that says the player whose ball is farthest from the hole plays first. Today, the Royal and Ancient Golf Club of St. Andrews oversees the worldwide rules of golf from its office in Scotland.

Coming to the United States

Golf was still a sport limited to a small group of rich people during the 1700s. People in the United States knew little about the game in the 1770s. There is evidence, however, that golf had made its way across the Atlantic Ocean. Dr. Benjamin Rush was the first to write about golf in the United States.

Rush was one of the 56 men who signed the Declaration of Independence in 1776. He also helped Meriwether Lewis prepare for the Lewis and Clark expedition in 1803. Rush was introduced to golf before both of those historical moments.

Rush studied medicine at the University of Edinburgh in

ROYAL BLACKHEATH GOLF CLUB

While St. Andrews is considered the home of golf, Royal Blackheath Golf Club in London, England, has a place in golf history, too. In 1603, King James VI of Scotland assumed the throne of England, becoming James I of England. He brought golf with him. James I and his entourage turned the land at Blackheath into a golf course. Golf at Blackheath began somewhere between 1603 and 1608. Today, Royal Blackheath Golf Club is known as the oldest membership club in the world.

Scotland. During his several years in Europe he learned about the game. In 1772, he was back in the United States. Rush wrote a document titled, "Sermons to Gentlemen upon Temperance and Exercise." In that document, he listed golf as a way for men to gain better health. Because golf was unknown to many, he explained the game to his readers:

> Golf is an exercise which is much used by the Gentlemen in Scotland. A large common in which there are several little holes is chosen for the purpose. It is played with little leather balls stuffed with feathers; and sticks made somewhat in the form of a bandy-wicket. He who puts a ball into a given number of holes, with the fewest strokes, gets the game. The late Dr. McKenzie, Author of the essay on Health and Long Life, used to say, that a man would live ten years the longer for using this exercise once or twice a week.

HITTING THE LINKS

Many golf courses are called "links-style courses." Links-style courses are patterned after the earliest courses from Scotland. They are usually built close to the coast on rough, sandy terrain that "links" the coast to the more fertile farmland. A non-links course, therefore, is generally built inland on more stable ground. Early links-style courses in Scotland used grazing sheep to keep the grass cut short. Although most courses are non-links courses, especially in the United States, golfers often use the term "hitting the links" when talking about going to play a round of golf.

THE BRITISH OPEN

The British Open is one of the most difficult tournaments to win because it is always played on a links course in England or Scotland. The tournament rotates every year between several different courses. All of them are built on rough ground, which makes play difficult for the players. The British Open is usually played on a course near the coast. That means cooler temperatures, rainy weather, and tough winds are usually a factor.

With the exception of a few players here and there, golf did not gain much attention in the United States until the 1880s. Around the world, however, golf's popularity exploded in the 1800s.

A Global Game

The United Kingdom (UK) is a group of united areas that consists of England, Northern Ireland, Scotland, and Wales. It had less than 10 golf clubs in 1800. But by 1900, there were more than 2,300 golf clubs in the UK.

The sport had become so popular in the UK that, in 1860, the Open Championship was established. Most people in the United States know the tournament today as the British Open. Eight professionals competed at the first British Open. It was played on October 17, 1860, at Prestwick Golf Club in Scotland. The tournament featured three rounds of 12 holes each. Willie Park

Golf legend Tom Morris Sr. was commonly referred to as Old Tom Morris to avoid confusion with his son, Tom Morris Jr., another great golfer.

won the title by just 2 strokes over Old Tom Morris. Park was awarded the Challenge Belt. It went to every winner of the Open from 1860 to 1871. In 1872, the prize was changed to a claret jug. The claret jug has been awarded to every winner since.

Golf was not just a UK sport, though. During the 1800s, golf began to expand into other parts of the world. The Royal Calcutta Golf Club was built in 1829 in India. It was the first golf club outside of the UK. During the next several decades, golf clubs were built in Australia, China, France, Japan, South Africa, and Thailand.

North America's first club was the Royal Montreal Golf Club in Quebec, Canada. It was built in 1873. The United States would get its first club a few years later.

TOM MORRIS, OLD AND YOUNG

One of the first great champions in golf history was Old Tom Morris. He was born in St. Andrews, Scotland—the home of golf. Morris helped to create the British Open in 1860. He won four of the first eight Opens and finished second twice. He played his last Open in 1896, at the age of 76. His son, Young Tom Morris, was also a great champion. Like his father, Young Tom won the Open four times. His first win came when he was just 17 years old. He later became the first person to win it three years in a row. Young Tom died of a heart attack in 1875 at the age of 24, shortly after his wife and baby died during childbirth.

CHAPTER 3

A WORLDWIDE GAME

Golf took a while to gain popularity in the United States. Benjamin Rush wrote about the game during the 1770s—before the United States gained its independence. Yet only a small amount of people around the United States played golf throughout the next 100 years. It was not until the 1890s that golf took off in the United States.

Scotland native John Reid immigrated to the United States and worked at J. L. Mott Iron Works in New York City. Being from Scotland, he was also a golfer. One of Reid's friends, Robert Lockhart, visited Scotland and brought back a gift to Reid. Lockhart gave his friend six golf clubs and two dozen golf balls. He had purchased them from golf legend Old Tom Morris.

Old Tom Morris once used this putter. It was sold at auction in 2005.

Using his new clubs and balls, Reid first played golf in the United States in February 1888. He and his friends created three short holes in a cow pasture in Yonkers, New York. Two months later, they created a six-hole course in the same town. Later, they moved the club to a bigger piece of land. This land included an apple orchard. That led to the group becoming known as the Apple Tree Gang.

Reid also helped to establish the St. Andrew's Golf Club just north of New York City in 1888. It is the oldest golf club in the United States. And it was named after the famous course in Scotland, which is the oldest in the world. For that, Reid is often referred to as the Father of American Golf.

The St. Andrew's Golf Club was one of the founding clubs for the United States Golf Association (USGA) in 1888. The USGA establishes and interprets rules for golf in the United States. It works with the Royal and Ancient Golf Club of

A GENTLEMAN'S GAME

For years, golf was considered a game for "gentlemen." Affluent players took pride in how well they dressed for a round of golf. Their clothing generally set them apart from the less affluent players. Gentlemen often wore shirts and ties on the course. They would also wear sport coats or sweaters. Many times, affluent players looked down upon those who were not considered "gentlemen."

St. Andrews, which oversees the rules worldwide. The USGA also holds several national championships every year. Among those tournaments are the US Open for men and the US Women's Open. It also holds national championships for the best amateur players (players who are not paid), and the best junior (under 18) and senior (age 50-plus) players.

Reid's six-hole course in Yonkers was one of the few courses in the United States in 1888. Just 12 years later in 1900, the United States had more than 1,000 golf courses. Golf was clearly becoming a popular sport in America.

Golf around the Globe

Men and women, old and young, could participate in

PAR FOR THE COURSE

When scoring a round of golf, players often aim to shoot "par." That is the number of strokes it should take for a top golfer to complete the course. A standard course has a par of 72, but some courses have different par totals. The use of the term "par" dates back to the late 1800s. US women might have been the first to use a scoring system in relation to par, in the 1890s. US men soon followed. Golfers try to keep their score at par or better. The best golfers often score well below par.

Scoring for a particular hole:

- Ace – Hole in 1 from the teeing area
- Double eagle – 3 strokes under par
- Eagle – 2 strokes under par
- Birdie – 1 stroke under par
- Par – Even par, the expected score for an elite golfer
- Bogey – 1 stroke over par
- Double bogey – 2 strokes over par
- Triple bogey – 3 strokes over par

golf. That helped the sport spread quickly around the world. Australia, New Zealand, and Sweden were among the many other countries to see a boom in golf. Golf was becoming big in South Africa, too.

In 1892, golf clubs from around South Africa met in Kimberley, the capital of Northern Cape. Just three clubs showed up—Kimberley, Cape Town, and Port Elizabeth. Still, golfers from those clubs competed in the first national amateur championship that year. The next year, several other clubs showed up. The success and stature of the tournament grew in the following years. The South African Open was established in 1903 and played in Port Elizabeth.

The South African Golf Union (SAGU) was formed in 1910. However, only white players could be members. The country was segregated at the time. Later, black players formed the South African Golf Association (SAGA). In 1992,

LADIES PLAY, TOO

As golf grew around the world, women began to love the sport. Many golf courses denied women the right to play. Therefore, women formed their own golf clubs. In 1895, Lucy Barnes Brown won the first US Women's Amateur Championship. Beatrix Hoyt won three straight US Women's Amateur titles from 1896 to 1898. Her first championship came when she was just 16 years old. The Ladies Professional Golf Association was founded in 1950. As of 2011, there are 33 women enshrined in the World Golf Hall of Fame in St. Augustine, Florida.

Nicknamed "The Black Knight," Gary Player of South Africa was the only modern player to win the British Open in three different decades.

the SAGU and SAGA merged. Since 1997, it has been known as the SAGA. It continues to govern the sport in that country.

South Africa might not be the most well-known location for golf. Several great players have come from there, though. Bobby Locke was a whiz with the putter. He won the British Open four times through the 1950s. Gary Player turned pro in 1953. He won nine major championships and was inducted into the World Golf Hall of Fame in 1974. Ernie Els was the PGA Tour's Rookie of the Year in 1994. He also won two US Opens, a British Open, and is in the Hall of Fame. Nick Price won three major championships and is in the World Golf Hall of Fame.

Francis Ouimet, *center*, defeated British legends Harry Vardon, *left*, and Ted Ray, *right*, in 1913 to become the first amateur to win the US Open.

The US Open and PGA Championship

Meanwhile, golf was becoming a major sport in the United States. The US Open was first played in 1895 in Newport, Rhode Island. There were just 11 entries that year. In 2011, the USGA said 8,300 golfers entered for the chance to win the US Open. Since 1895, the tournament has been held every year except during World War I (1917 and 1918) and World War II (1942 through 1945). It has been one of the premier golf events in the United States during that time.

The PGA was founded in 1916 to organize all professional golfers. Unlike the USGA, the PGA does not set rules for golf. Instead, it organizes the golfers who are paid to teach and manage the game. Originally, those who played the game professionally were a part of the PGA. However, they broke away from the organization in the late 1960s to form the PGA Tour. The PGA Tour is a series of golf tournaments played each year in which players earn prize money.

The biggest PGA event every year is the PGA Championship. The tournament was first held in 1916. Today it is one of the four majors. Like the US Open, the PGA Championship was canceled in 1917 and 1918 because of World War I. It was also cancelled in 1943 due to World War II. The PGA Championship has been played every other year since 1919. The US Open and the PGA Championship are two of the majors.

Not everyone loved golf. Famous author Mark Twain once said that golf "is a good walk spoiled." But despite that opinion, the game was becoming a hit around the world.

A GOLF PIONEER

Charles Blair Macdonald was born in the United States, but he learned about golf while studying at St. Andrews University in Scotland. In 1892, Macdonald founded the Chicago Golf Club in Wheaton, Illinois. It was originally just six holes. The course later became the first 18-hole course in the United States. Macdonald is known as the "Father of Golf Architecture." He designed many courses in the United States. He also sparked the creation of the USGA. Macdonald was the winner at the first US Amateur Championship, in 1895.

CHAPTER 4

STARS EMERGE

As golf grew in popularity, players got better. Some players became great. Old Tom Morris from Scotland was one of the first great players in golf's history. He won the British Open four times during the 1800s. Harry Vardon became a golf legend during the 1890s and early 1900s. He was born in Jersey, a British territory just off the coast of France. Vardon won the British Open six times from 1896 to 1914. Through 2011, Vardon was the only player to win the event more than five times. Vardon was also the first British golfer to win the US Open. He won that event in 1900.

Walter Hagen was one of the first true American golf legends. Born in New York, Hagen won 11 major championships during his career. He was just 21 years old when he won his first major,

Harry Vardon won the British Open six times. That remained a record through 2011.

Walter Hagen, *left*, was the first US-born British Open winner. Gene Sarazen, *right*, completed the first career Grand Slam.

the 1914 US Open. In 1922, he became the first US-born player to win the British Open. Hagen won the British Open three more times.

"I think Walter Hagen contributed more to golf than any player today or ever," said fellow US golfer Gene Sarazen. "He took the game all over the world. He popularized it here and everywhere. Walter was at the head of the class."

That is quite a compliment coming from Sarazen. He was a golf legend in his own right. Sarazen won seven major titles during his career. He was the US Open champion in 1922 and 1932. Sarazen was also known for his stylish clothing and for inventing the sand wedge. That is a club that helps golfers get their ball out of the sand bunkers. He introduced the club during the 1932 British Open, which he won.

Hagen won his last major title at the 1929 British Open. Sarazen won his final major in 1935, at the second playing of the Masters. He won after he holed his second shot for a double eagle (3 under par) on the par-5 15th hole in the final round. The shot was called "the shot heard 'round the world."

Bobby Jones was another one of the game's greats, although he never played professional golf. Jones entered 20 major tournaments as an amateur from 1923 to 1930. He won 13 of them. Jones did not play golf full-time. While he was winning major titles, he was also a stellar student. He earned college degrees from Harvard and Georgia Tech. He also attended law school at Emory and passed the bar exam before graduation. That is a test prospective lawyers must take to earn certification.

At age 28, Jones retired from golf to become a lawyer. That was after he won the unprecedented Grand Slam in 1930. The Grand Slam refers to winning all four major championships in one year. Jones later founded and helped to design Augusta National Golf Club. That course opened in 1933 and has hosted the Masters every year since 1934, with the exception of three during World War II.

Passing the Torch

A new group of stars came aboard after Hagen, Jones, and Sarazen. Byron Nelson might have had the greatest single season of any player in golf history. In 1945, the Texan won 18 tournaments. At one point that season, Nelson won 11 tournaments in a row. Both were still PGA Tour records in 2011. A five-time major champion, Nelson won a total of 52 PGA Tour events during his career.

Ben Hogan grew up with Nelson in Fort Worth, Texas. Like his friend, Hogan went on to become a golf legend. But before he could do that, Hogan had to battle himself. When he was young, his swing produced a bad hook. A hook is when the ball starts out to the right but flies way to the left and misses the target. Hogan worked hard to improve his swing and became one of the greatest technical golfers of all time. With his masterful swing, Hogan won nine major championships from 1946 to 1953.

Hogan suffered a near-fatal auto accident in 1949. His car collided with a bus on a foggy day. That put Hogan's career in jeopardy, but he won six of his majors after the accident.

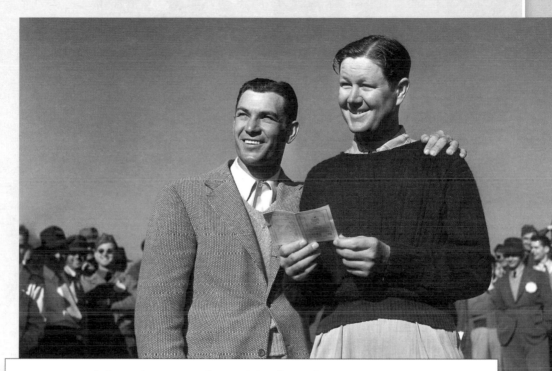

Ben Hogan, *left*, and Byron Nelson, *right*, forced a playoff during the 1942 Masters. Both golfers once caddied at the same country club in Texas.

Nelson and Hogan had company at the top of the golf world. Sam Snead of Virginia won a record 82 PGA Tour tournaments during his career. As of 2011, he still held the record for victories. Snead was a seven-time winner in major tournaments. But one of his greatest contributions to golf came later in his career. Snead helped to develop the Senior Tour, which is now called the Champions Tour. It allows players aged 50 and over to compete against each other professionally.

THE BABE

Babe Didrikson Zaharias was a great athlete, no matter what sport she tried. An All-American in basketball, she also won two gold medals in track and field at the 1932 Olympic Games in Los Angeles, California. She was also exceptional in baseball, boxing, diving, swimming, tennis, and other sports. "My goal was to be the greatest athlete who ever lived," she said.

During the 1932 Olympic Games, Didrikson Zaharias played a round of golf for the first time and shot a 91. It was not long before she was the most dominant women's player in the game.

In 1946, as an amateur, she won a reported 16 consecutive tournaments. She turned pro in 1947 and helped create the LPGA in 1950. Didrikson Zaharias went on to win 31 LPGA events, including the US Women's Open three times. Didrikson Zaharias was named by the Associated Press as the Greatest Female Athlete of the first half of the twentieth century. She died of cancer in 1956.

Women Break In

Women have played golf nearly as long as men. Mary, Queen of Scots was one of the first women to pick up golf clubs, back in the 1500s. The women's game grew in popularity throughout the years. By the 1930s and 1940s, Mildred "Babe" Didrikson Zaharias and Patty Berg were among the elite players in women's golf.

Thanks to pioneers such as Didrikson Zaharias and Berg, women's golf grew large enough to demand organization. They were part of the group of 13 women who established the Ladies Professional Golf Association (LPGA) in 1950. Much like the PGA Tour, it organizes the women's professional game and schedule.

Patty Berg, *left*, and Mildred "Babe" Didrikson Zaharias, *right*, helped to establish the LPGA in 1950.

Today, the LPGA is home of the LPGA Tour. It features the best female players in the world in a series of tournaments throughout the year. Women's golf also has four majors, like the men. Unlike the men's majors, however, the women's majors have changed over the years. In 2011 they were the Kraft Nabisco Championship, the LPGA Championship, the US Women's Open, and the Women's British Open. A fifth major, the Evian Masters in France, is set to be added in 2013.

Since its creation, the LPGA has been home to many golf legends, including Didrikson Zaharias and Berg. During her career, which began in the 1930s, Berg won more major

STELLAR PLAYERS

Because Jack Nicklaus, Arnold Palmer, and Gary Player dominated the headlines, many other great players were overshadowed in the 1960s, 1970s, and 1980s. Among them was Severiano "Seve" Ballesteros of Spain. Through 2010, he had more European Tour wins (50) than anyone in history. He also won nine PGA Tour events and five majors from 1979 to 1988. Ballesteros died of cancer at age 54 in 2011.

Billy Casper's 51 PGA Tour wins rank him seventh all-time through 2011. He won three majors, including the 1970 Masters and the US Open twice. Hale Irwin was a three-time US Open champion. He has since made his mark in the Champions Tour (for players aged 50 and over). Irwin has more Champions wins (45) than anyone, and his seven Champions majors titles rank second to Nicklaus's eight. Lee Trevino won 29 PGA Tour events and six majors. Since turning 50, he has also won 29 Champions Tour events—second only to Irwin's 45.

championships (15) than any female player in history. Through 2011, her 60 wins rank fourth all-time.

Among the other top female players from the early days of the LPGA was US golfer Nancy Lopez. She turned professional in 1977 and won 48 LPGA events during her career. That included three wins in the LPGA Championship.

American Betsy Rawls won 55 tournaments from 1951 to 1972. Eight of those wins were in majors. Kathy Whitworth was the winningest LPGA player ever through 2011. She finished her career with 88 wins—more than any man—and six major titles. Mickey Wright had 82 career wins and won 13 major titles, mostly during the 1950s and 1960s.

Those still ranked second in LPGA history through 2011. Her golf swing has often been claimed to be the model swing for all golfers—men and women.

Golfers become TV Stars

Golf stardom hit a new level in the 1960s. That is when tournaments began to be broadcast on TV on a regular basis. All of a sudden, Arnold Palmer's popularity skyrocketed. Hundreds of fans nicknamed "Arnie's Army" followed the Pennsylvania native on the course. They loved him for his daring style. He would often attempt challenging shots that most golfers would avoid. Nicknamed "The King," Palmer was already a popular figure by 1960. He turned pro in 1954 and won the Masters in 1958, 1960, 1962, and 1964. The Masters broadcasts are among the most highly rated in sports. They started the popular trend of golf on television.

Palmer went on to win 62 PGA Tour events and seven major titles during his career. Perhaps his greatest moment came at the

US Open in 1960. At the start of the final round, Palmer was seven shots behind the leaders. But he drove the first green, a par 4, and made a charge to the top. He scored a 65 in the final round to win the tournament by two strokes.

The 1960 US Open was a landmark event. It connected golf's past (47-year-old Hogan was among the contenders), present (Palmer), and future. The future was Jack Nicklaus. A 20-year-old amateur at the time, he finished second to Palmer at the US Open.

The Golden Bear

Most regard Nicklaus as the greatest golfer ever. His results certainly suggest that. The Ohio native won 70 tournaments on the PGA Tour. He also won 18 major titles. Through 2011, that was more than anyone else in history. He also finished second in 19 majors. Nicklaus was nicknamed "The Golden Bear" for his blond hair and great size and strength.

Arnold Palmer takes a shot as fans look on during his 1961 British Open victory. Palmer earned a loyal fan base commonly called "Arnie's Army."

Aside from his results, Nicklaus grew famous for the way he played the game. He had power, but he also was precise with his putting. Nicklaus also knew how to manage a course like few before him. Nicklaus was so good that Bobby Jones once said, "He plays a game with which I am not familiar."

Nicklaus continued his winning ways after turning 50. Playing on the Senior Tour, Nicklaus won 10 tournaments and eight majors from 1990 to 1996. Palmer won five majors on the Senior Tour from 1980 to 1985. The way Palmer and Nicklaus played was enough to make them all-time greats. That they were great in front of a television audience made them more popular.

CHAPTER 5

GREAT MOMENTS AND HALLOWED GROUNDS

Jack Nicklaus was considered past his prime at the 1986 Masters. He was 46 years old and had not won a major tournament in six years. It did not look like Nicklaus was going to get a win at this tournament, either. Eight holes into the final round, Nicklaus was 6 strokes behind. It would take a miracle for him to win. He got that miracle. Nicklaus birdied holes 9, 10, 11, and 13. He then got an eagle on 15. The Golden Bear then birdied on 16 and 17. On 18, he completed the comeback and won the Masters for the sixth and final time. Nicklaus's caddie during that tournament was his son, Jack II.

In 2007, *Golf Magazine* named that comeback as the greatest moment in golf. The moment was made great not only because Nicklaus won. It was made great because of where it took place.

Jack Nicklaus celebrates his 1986 Masters victory at Augusta National. He became the oldest player to win the event.

The Pacific Ocean runs along the 18th hole at the Pebble Beach Golf Links.

The Masters is played every year at Augusta National Golf Club. The course has provided golf with some of the greatest moments in the sport's history. Tiger Woods became the youngest Masters champion in 1997. At age 21, he roared to a 12-shot victory at Augusta National. The win was especially significant as Woods became the first black player to win the tournament. He was also the first black player to win a major championship. It was Woods's first victory at a major and the beginning of his reign as the biggest star in golf.

But great players are not the only stars in golf. Many golf courses are as famous as the players. Because of the history involved with certain courses, they are considered hallowed grounds by many golf fans. Augusta National and the Old Course at St. Andrews, Scotland, are two of the most revered courses in all of golf. But they are not alone.

Pebble Beach

Pebble Beach Golf Links in California is one of the most majestic and beautiful courses in the world. Located on the West Coast, many of its holes have stellar views of Carmel Bay, which opens to the Pacific Ocean. The 18th hole at Pebble Beach is a long par-5 that is considered one of the great final holes in all of golf. It features the Pacific Ocean all along its left side.

Pebble Beach has hosted the US Open five times through 2011. One of those came in 1982. That is when Tom Watson had a remarkable finish to barely beat Nicklaus. Watson chipped in for birdie from deep rough on the next-to-last hole to move ahead of Nicklaus. Nicklaus had won the first US Open at

BREAKING THE BARRIER

Among the many great moments at Augusta National, the color barrier was broken there in 1975. Until 1961, the PGA had a rule that membership was only allowed for "professional golfers of the Caucasian race." That changed in 1961, when golfers of all races were allowed to play. And in 1975, Lee Elder became the first black player to qualify as a competitor in the Masters at Augusta National.

Pebble Beach in 1972. At the 2000 US Open, Woods was more dominant than any player in US Open history. He won by a stunning 15 strokes. Nobody had ever won a major tournament by that many strokes.

Making Pebble Beach even more attractive to golf fans is its other courses. Pebble Beach Golf Links is the most famous course in town. But the area also features Cypress Point Club and Spyglass Hill Golf Course. All three are considered to be among the most scenic and prestigious courses in the United States.

Oakmont

Oakmont Country Club in Oakmont, Pennsylvania, has also seen some of golf's greatest moments. Few courses in the United States are as difficult as Oakmont. It features 210 deep bunkers and greens that have hard surfaces, making for very speedy putts. Oakmont also has a championship history unmatched by most courses. The 2007 US Open was the eighth one played there.

AMERICA'S GREATEST?

Golf Digest and *Golf Magazine* have named Pine Valley Golf Club as the greatest golf course in United States for many years. Located in Pine Valley, New Jersey, it was built in 1918. It has never hosted a major professional tournament because it does not have enough room to fit all the spectators.

The Oakmont Country Club has hosted eight US Opens through 2011. No other course has hosted the tournament that many times.

Other major tournaments have been held there numerous times as well.

Perhaps Oakmont's signature moment came in 1973. At the US Open that summer, US golfer Johnny Miller fired an incredible 63 in the final round to win the tournament. He was 6 strokes back, in 13th place, when the final round started.

Oakmont was also the site of Nicklaus's first professional victory. He and Arnold Palmer were tied after 72 holes at the 1962 US Open. The course was not far from Palmer's hometown. In the 18-hole playoff to determine the winner, Nicklaus shot 71 to beat Palmer by three strokes.

THE GAME TODAY

Hundreds of years after golf got its start, the game is as strong as ever. Golf was once a game for wealthy white men in Scotland and England. For many years only "gentlemen," or the elite in society, played golf. But the sport has evolved. Today golf is enjoyed by a wide variety of people around the world. People of all races and of all classes play the game.

Perhaps no player is a better example of golf's growth than Eldrick "Tiger" Woods. He was born in 1975 in California. Woods's father, Earl, introduced Woods to golf by age two. The young boy appeared on a television talk show called the *Mike Douglas Show* in 1978 and putted against comedian Bob Hope. Woods won dozens of tournaments in his youth, including the Junior World Championships six times.

Tiger Woods has won every major championship at least three times. The only other player to do so through 2011 was Jack Nicklaus.

THE CADDIE

Most golfers carry their own golf bags around the course. Professional golfers, on the other hand, have caddies who do that for them. At professional tournaments, each player has a caddie. In addition to carrying the golfer's clubs, a caddie gives advice on what clubs to use, what hazards might be ahead, and helps to figure out how putts might break. Some golf courses offer caddies for average players, too.

Woods became a professional in 1996 and quickly changed the face of golf. Most golfers at the time were white. Woods, however, was part African American and part Asian. He became an inspiration to minority players.

While growing up, Woods decided he wanted to break Jack Nicklaus's record of winning 18 majors. He got an early start when he won the 1997 Masters at age 21. By the time he turned 30, Woods had won 10 major championships. His tremendous success—and his ability to dominate tournaments—made Woods perhaps the most famous athlete in the world.

Because of Woods, participation in golf increased among minorities and youths. According to the National Golf Foundation, there was a dramatic increase in participation among African Americans from 1991 to 1996—the year Woods became a professional. The overall number of junior golfers also increased by 34 percent from 1991 to 1996.

Throughout the early 2000s, Woods and Phil Mickelson entertained crowds with their rivalry. The two players' skills and charisma helped draw fans who normally would not be interested in golf. With Woods, many people came to see him because they believed he might be the greatest golfer to ever play.

In 2001, he became the first golfer in the modern era (1934 to the present) to hold the titles for all four majors at the same time. This became known as the "Tiger Slam." It would have been the Grand Slam had he won them all in the same year. But Woods won the 2000 US Open, British Open, and PGA Championship, and the 2001 Masters to start the next season.

Through 2011, Bobby Jones is the only player to have achieved the Grand Slam. He won the US Open, the US Amateur, the British Open, and the British Amateur in 1930. Those tournaments made up the Grand Slam prior

A GOLFER'S HANDICAP

Golfers who play regularly and record their scores are given a handicap number. The handicap is a golfer's average score in relation to par and using the course rating as a guide. The course rating is determined by the difficulty of the course. For example, if a golfer typically finishes 15 strokes over par, he or she has an approximate handicap of 15. Golfers that typically finish at par or below par are considered "scratch" golfers, with no handicap number. Handicaps allow golfers of varying handicaps to compete against each other during a round.

SORENSTAM LEADS THE PACK

For nearly 20 years, Annika Sorenstam was the best player on the LPGA Tour. The Swedish-born Sorenstam retired in 2008 with 93 professional victories. Her 72 LPGA wins ranked third all-time, and she finished with 10 major championships. She won the US Women's Open three times. She also gained a great deal of attention for competing against men in a PGA Tour event in 2003—the first woman to do that since 1945.

"She took it to the ultimate," said LPGA veteran Meg Mallon. "It's how long she lasted in that top spot that is most impressive from a player's perspective."

Sorenstam received great competition from many players, including Karrie Webb, who had 38 wins and seven majors as of 2011. Juli Inkster (31 wins, seven majors), Se Ri Pak (25 wins, five majors), and Lorena Ochoa (27 wins, two majors) were also among the best women's players of the 1990s and 2000s.

to the formation of the Masters Tournament in 1934.

Injuries and off-course issues slowed down Woods after he won the 2008 US Open. Through 2011, that was his last major championship victory. But with 14 total, he is still second only to Nicklaus. Many believe he could surpass the Golden Bear's record.

Stars of Today

By 2011, golf's popularity among young players was making an impact on the pro tours. South Africa's Charl Schwartzel won the Masters in 2011 at age 26. Germany's Martin Kaymer won the 2010 PGA Championship at 25 years old. And South African Louis Oosthuizen won the 2010 British Open at age 27.

Rory McIlroy, a 22-year-old from Northern Ireland, shot 16-under par to win the 2011 US Open. His score was a tournament record.

Rory McIlroy, a 22-year-old from Northern Ireland, was another young player who was showing signs of dominance in 2011. At the Masters, he entered the final round with a 4-stroke lead before collapsing. He finished 10 strokes behind the winner and tied for 15th place. But at the next major, the US Open, McIlroy won his first major in dominating fashion. His 72-hole score of 16-under par surpassed the previous US Open record of 12-under, which Woods had set in 2000.

The LPGA featured many young stars, as well. Among them were Paula Creamer, Morgan Pressel, Michelle Wie, and Yani Tseng. Creamer, who turned 25 in 2011, came into that season

Yani Tseng won the 2011 Women's British Open at age 22, becoming the youngest golfer to win five majors.

with nine career wins and 33 top-three finishes. Pressel first competed in the US Women's Open as a 12-year-old in 2001. Then, in 2005, she nearly won that tournament as a 17-year-old amateur. In 2007 she won the Kraft Nabisco Championship, earning her first major.

Wie has been on the path to stardom since she was a little girl. The Hawaii native was one of the best amateur players in the United States before becoming a teenager. She turned pro at age 16. Just 21 years old in 2011, she came into the season with two LPGA wins under her belt.

Tseng of Taiwan became the youngest female golfer in history to win four major titles in 2011. She shot a final-round 66 to capture the 2011 LPGA Championship by 10 strokes. Tseng, who was only 22 at the time, already was the youngest player in LPGA history to win three majors. She had previously won the 2008 LPGA Championship, the 2010 Kraft Nabisco Championship, and the 2010 Women's British Open. Tseng was not done yet. She then won the 2011 Women's British Open. That made her the youngest golfer in history to win five major titles.

Advances in Technology

As the game developed, so did the equipment. New technology has made golf clubs and golf balls better than ever. For years, golf clubs were made with wood shafts. Today, clubs are made from

GOLF EXPLODES IN ASIA

During the twentieth century and into the twenty-first century, golf became a major sport in Asia. In particular, Japan, South Korea, and China have seen thousands of golf courses built in the past 100 years. The Japan Golf Tour was established in 1973, and the Asian Tour was established in 1995. As of 2011, many of the world's best golfers are Asian-born. On the LPGA, Na Yeon Choi and Jiyai Shin of South Korea finished one-two on the 2010 prize money list. Several other Asian players were among the top 20. On the PGA Tour, Asian golfers also were becoming prominent. South Korea's Y. E. Yang outdueled Tiger Woods to win the 2009 PGA Championship. And South Korea's K. J. Choi won the 2011 Players Championship, one of the most coveted PGA Tour tournaments.

different types of metal, including steel, titanium, and aluminum. The equipment is designed to help golfers hit the ball farther and with more accuracy.

Rather than carrying their bags around the course for several hours, average golfers now strap their clubs to a cart and drive around. Professional golfers are still required to walk, but they have a caddie to carry their clubs for them. Caddies are paid to carry clubs and consult with golfers at professional tournaments and at some larger golf courses.

Another advance in golf technology is the use of video. Many golfers videotape their swings and then review the tape. This allows players a chance to see flaws in their swings and then correct those flaws. All of that technology has helped the level of play among the average golfer rise in recent years.

Looking Forward

Through hundreds of years of play and countless changes to the game, the purity of the game of golf is still intact. Golf is

Golf might be one of the oldest sports, but the future is bright.

still a game that prides itself on its course etiquette and player honesty. It is also a game that takes great pride in its tradition. More than most sports, the tradition of golf is rich.

One other aspect of golf remains the same today as it was in the 1400s: it is not an easy game. No matter how much the players and the equipment have changed, the game is still one that humbles players. Even the best players of today walk off the course knowing they could have done better. For many, that is what keeps them coming back for more.

TIMELINE

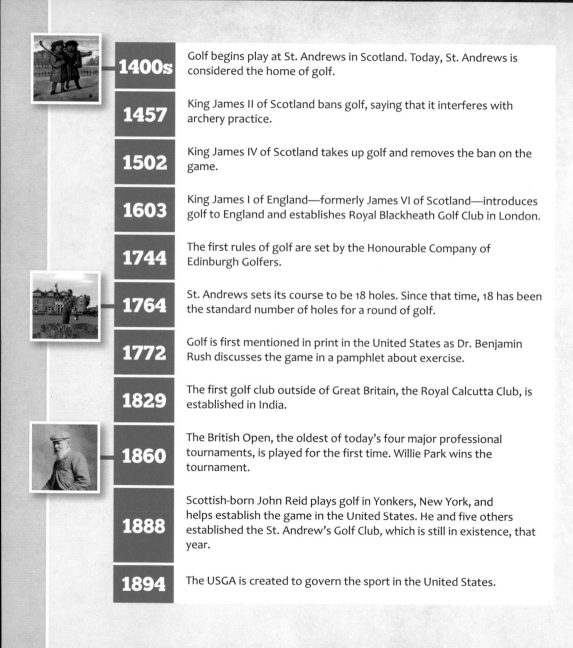

1400s Golf begins play at St. Andrews in Scotland. Today, St. Andrews is considered the home of golf.

1457 King James II of Scotland bans golf, saying that it interferes with archery practice.

1502 King James IV of Scotland takes up golf and removes the ban on the game.

1603 King James I of England—formerly James VI of Scotland—introduces golf to England and establishes Royal Blackheath Golf Club in London.

1744 The first rules of golf are set by the Honourable Company of Edinburgh Golfers.

1764 St. Andrews sets its course to be 18 holes. Since that time, 18 has been the standard number of holes for a round of golf.

1772 Golf is first mentioned in print in the United States as Dr. Benjamin Rush discusses the game in a pamphlet about exercise.

1829 The first golf club outside of Great Britain, the Royal Calcutta Club, is established in India.

1860 The British Open, the oldest of today's four major professional tournaments, is played for the first time. Willie Park wins the tournament.

1888 Scottish-born John Reid plays golf in Yonkers, New York, and helps establish the game in the United States. He and five others established the St. Andrew's Golf Club, which is still in existence, that year.

1894 The USGA is created to govern the sport in the United States.

1895	The US Open, the US Amateur, and the US Women's Amateur tournaments are played for the first time.
1916	The PGA of America is founded.
1947	The final round of the US Open is broadcast on television. It is the first time golf is shown on US TV.
1950	The LPGA is formed.
1961	For the first time, the PGA of America allows non-Caucasians to be members.
1986	Jack Nicklaus wins the Masters. It is his 18th major championship, a record that still stood in 2011.
1996	Tiger Woods, one of the world's greatest amateurs ever, turns pro at age 21.
1997	Woods wins the Masters, becoming the first African American to do so. It was the first major title for Woods.
2001	With a victory in the Masters, Woods becomes the first player in the modern era to hold all four major titles. It is dubbed the "Tiger Slam."
2011	Rory McIlroy, a 22-year-old from Northern Ireland, wins the US Open. His final score of 16-under par is the best score in the 111-year history of the event.
2011	Yani Tseng, a 22-year-old from Taiwan, becomes the youngest woman to win five major championships when she captures the Women's British Open.

LEGENDS OF GOLF

 MEN

Walter Hagen	**Byron Nelson**	**Sam Snead**
USA	USA	USA
Ben Hogan	**Jack Nicklaus**	**Lee Trevino**
USA	USA	USA
Bobby Jones	**Arnold Palmer**	**Harry Vardon**
USA	USA	England
Phil Mickelson	**Gary Player**	**Tom Watson**
USA	South Africa	USA
Tom Morris Sr.	**Gene Sarazen**	**Eldrick "Tiger" Woods**
Scotland	USA	USA

WOMEN

Patty Berg	**Betsy Rawls**	**Kathy Whitworth**
USA	USA	USA
Nancy Lopez	**Annika Sorenstam**	**Mary Kathryn "Mickey" Wright**
USA	Sweden	USA
Lorena Ochoa	**Louise Suggs**	**Mildred "Babe" Didrikson Zaharias**
Mexico	USA	USA

GLOSSARY

affluent
Having a lot of wealth.

amateur
A player who is not paid to compete.

birdie
A golfer scores a birdie when he or she scores 1 under par for the hole.

bunker
In golf, a bunker is an obstacle, such as a patch of sand or mound of dirt.

caddie
A person who is paid to carry clubs for a golfer and offer advice during a round of golf.

etiquette
Standard requirements for social behavior.

founded
In terms of a golf course or club, it means the creation of that golf course or club.

Grand Slam
Winning all four majors in one season or in a career.

green
The area nearest to the hole. Putts are played here.

hallowed
Highly respected or revered.

handicap
A golfer's average score in relation to par and using the course rating.

links
Areas of rough terrain that connect the coast to the farmland. Many golf courses in Great Britain are built on this land.

majestic
Possessing dignity or grand qualities.

par
The number of strokes it should take for an elite golfer to complete a course or an individual hole.

prestigious
Having a high reputation.

segregated
When groups of people are separated because of race, ethnic background, race, or other characteristics.

terrain
Physical features of a piece of land.

FOR MORE INFORMATION

Selected Bibliography

Fimrite, Ron. "Sir Walter." *SI Vault*. Turner-SI Digital. 19 June 1989. Web. 7 Sept. 2011.

"Previous Opens." *The Open Championship*. R&A Championships Limited. n.d. Web. 7 Sept. 2011.

Uschan, Michael V. *History of Sports: Golf*. San Diego, CA: Lucent Books, 2001. Print.

Further Readings

Cook, Kevin, ed. *The Golf Book*. New York: Sports Illustrated Books, 2009. Print.

Gordon, John. *The Kids Book of Golf*. Tonawanda, N.Y.: Kids Can Press, 2001. Print.

McCormick, David, and Charles McGrath, eds. *The Ultimate Golf Book*. Boston, MA: Houghton Mifflin, 2002. Print.

Mickelson, Phil. *One Magical Sunday (But Winning Isn't Everything)*. New York: Time Warner Book Group, 2007. Print.

Nicklaus, Jack. *Golf My Way*. New York: Simon & Schuster, 2005. Print.

Web Links

To learn more about golf, visit ABDO Publishing Company online at **www.abdopublishing.com**. Web sites about golf are featured on our Book Links page. These links are routinely monitored and updated to provide the most current information available.

Places to Visit

USGA Museum

77 Liberty Corner Road, Bernards Township, NJ 07931
(908) 234-2300
www.usgamuseum.com
This museum features a large collection of golf artifacts and memorabilia. A series of interactive and multimedia exhibits chronicles the growth and development of golf in the United States. Visitors can also try their luck on an old-fashioned putting green.

World Golf Hall of Fame

One World Golf Place, St. Augustine, FL 32092
(904) 940-4123
www.worldgolfhalloffame.org
This hall of fame and museum features exhibits that chronicle the history of golf as well as hands-on activities for visitors to learn more about the sport. Tickets to the hall of fame also include access to an IMAX film and an 18-hole putting course.

INDEX

About the Author

Brian Howell is a freelance writer based in Colorado. He has a bachelor's degree in journalism with a minor in history. He has had several books published about sports and history. He lives with his wife and four children in his native Colorado.